A Congress WBN Publication

Produced By:

 and

DISCOVERING God TOGETHER

Discovery Workbook #6

THIS BOOK BELONGS TO:
_____

About the WE MAGNIFY YOU Discovery Workbook Series

Our families are at the core of our Kingdom Communities. The WE MAGNIFY YOU album provides us with a wonderful opportunity to develop and strengthen the expression of worship in our homes.

Each We Magnify You Discovery Workbook has been designed for parents, guardians, teachers and children to experience and explore the songs together.

Discover new sight of what it means to magnify, exalt and praise our God. Together, our families will develop a deeper and stronger understanding of who God is, releasing a whole-hearted expression of worship unto Him.

For each song on the WE MAGNIFY YOU album, we have a Workbook with the lyrics and specially created activities.

Enjoy taking time together to consider what the lyrics mean. Explore scripture verses that tell us more about each song. Engage in fun activities, including word puzzles and coloring games.

Through it all we can together gain a deeper understanding of how the words we sing reflect the lives we must live, as we align ourselves to God.

Now that is a beautiful thing!

Guidance for Parents

The WE MAGNIFY YOU worship album from Congress MusicFactory contains prayers and songs from Dr. Woodroffe and saints from Elijah Centre and Kingdom Communities across Congress WBN.

WE MAGNIFY YOU is a powerful expression of worship and praise to our Lord. Each workbook in the We Magnify You Discovery Series explores the lyrics of the songs, sharing explanations, key scriptures and fun activities.

These resources will help us to align our lives, our families and our communities to the words that we lift unto God.

HOLY IS THE LAMB

LYRICS

Holy, Holy,
Holy is the Lamb
Lord God Almighty
Who was and is
Who was and is
Who was and is to come

All creation gives You glory
With all our hearts we bless Your Name
From every language, tribe and nation
Your holy people sing Your praise

We bow before Your holy presence
We lift our hands and worship You
Lord, You alone deserve this honor
You alone deserve all praise
All praise

WE MAGNIFY YOU Discovery Workbook Series

Activity Time

Read, color and learn the verse below:

Holy, holy, holy is the Lord God Almighty, who was, and is, and is to come."

Revelation 4:8

Holy, Holy, Holy is the Lamb

Jesus is the Lamb of God!

A lamb is a young sheep—but what does Jesus have in common with a sheep?

Long ago, people honored God by giving Him their best lamb. They would place the lamb on an altar as a sacrifice—to say sorry for their sins, or to let God know how thankful they were about something.

Holy means sacred and set apart for a special purpose. The lamb was the perfect sacrifice, because it represented something that was pure, innocent and precious.

Jesus is the **Holy Lamb** because He was without sin; He was innocent. He gave His life as a sacrifice for us so that all who believe in Him and follow His ways could enter the Kingdom of God.

Can you unscramble these words? Do you know what they mean?

Ask a grown up for help if you need to!

LFOYGRI

_ _ _ _ _ _ _

ONROH

_ _ _ _ _

ROETHN

_ _ _ _ _ _

XTEAL

_ _ _ _ _

NRGIE

_ _ _ _ _

ERVROEF

_ _ _ _ _ _ _

ANSWER: GLORIFY, HONOR, THRONE, EXALT, REIGN, FOREVER

BOOK 6: Holy is the Lamb

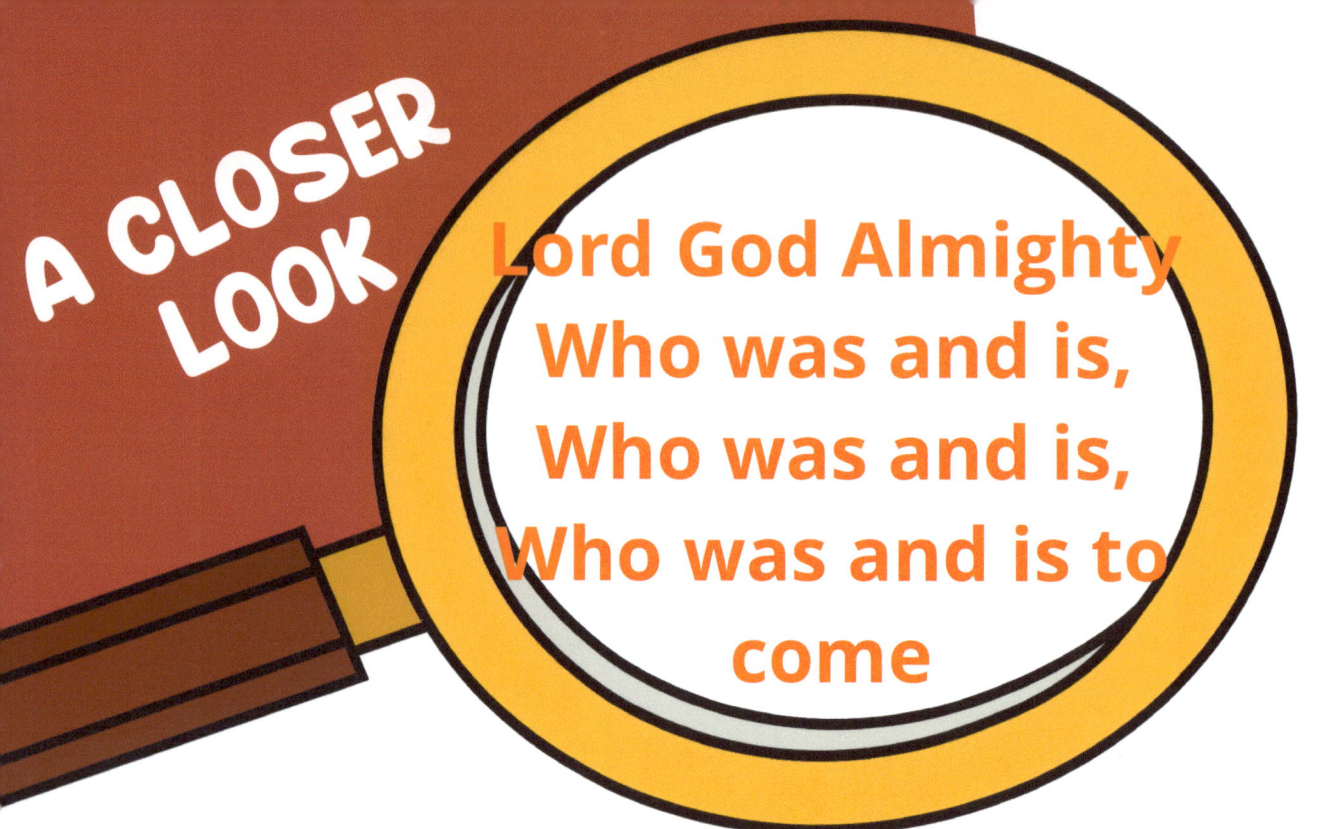

Our Lord is the **Lord God Almighty!**

That means He is stronger than the strongest super heroes, and more powerful than the world's most powerful armies. He can defeat any enemy! No one is stronger or more powerful than Him!

Who was, and is and is to come simply means that God existed before we were born; He is with us today, and He will be with us tomorrow. In fact, He is eternal. That means He will be around forever!

God does not exist in time like us.

In the first box below, draw a picture of yourself when you were younger. Then draw yourself now in the second box. Next, imagine how you might look in the future and draw the future you in box #3.

God doesn't have to imagine the future, He knows it already!

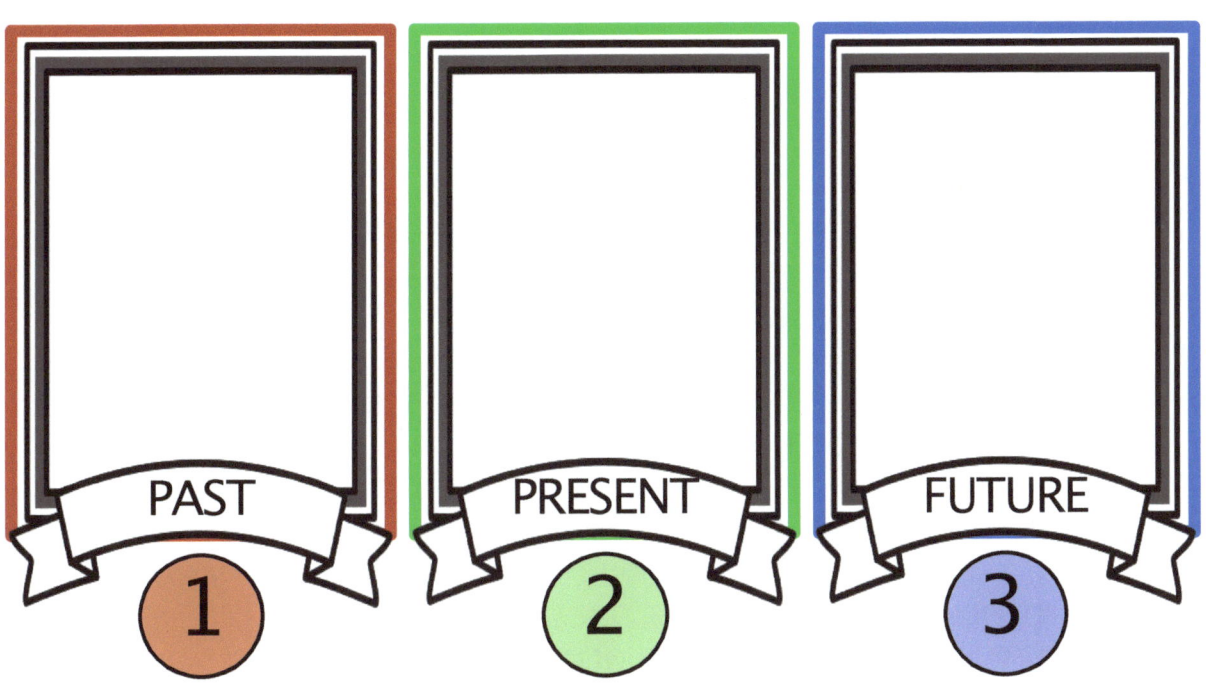

Revelation 1:8

"I am the First and the Last," says the Lord God Almighty, who is, who was, and who is to come.

Creation is everything God has made, like the sky, stars, plants, rivers, insects, birds, animals and trees. God made all of this!

When we look at creation and see the beauty of a flower in bloom, or how animals hunt, or how birds soar in the sky... we can see how awesome God, our creator, is!

In other words, **God's creation gives Him glory,** just like we do in our worship.

Everything on earth will worship You; they will sing Your praises, shouting Your name in glorious songs.

Psalm 66:4

Activity Time

Can you find your way from the Beginning (ALPHA) to the End (OMEGA)?

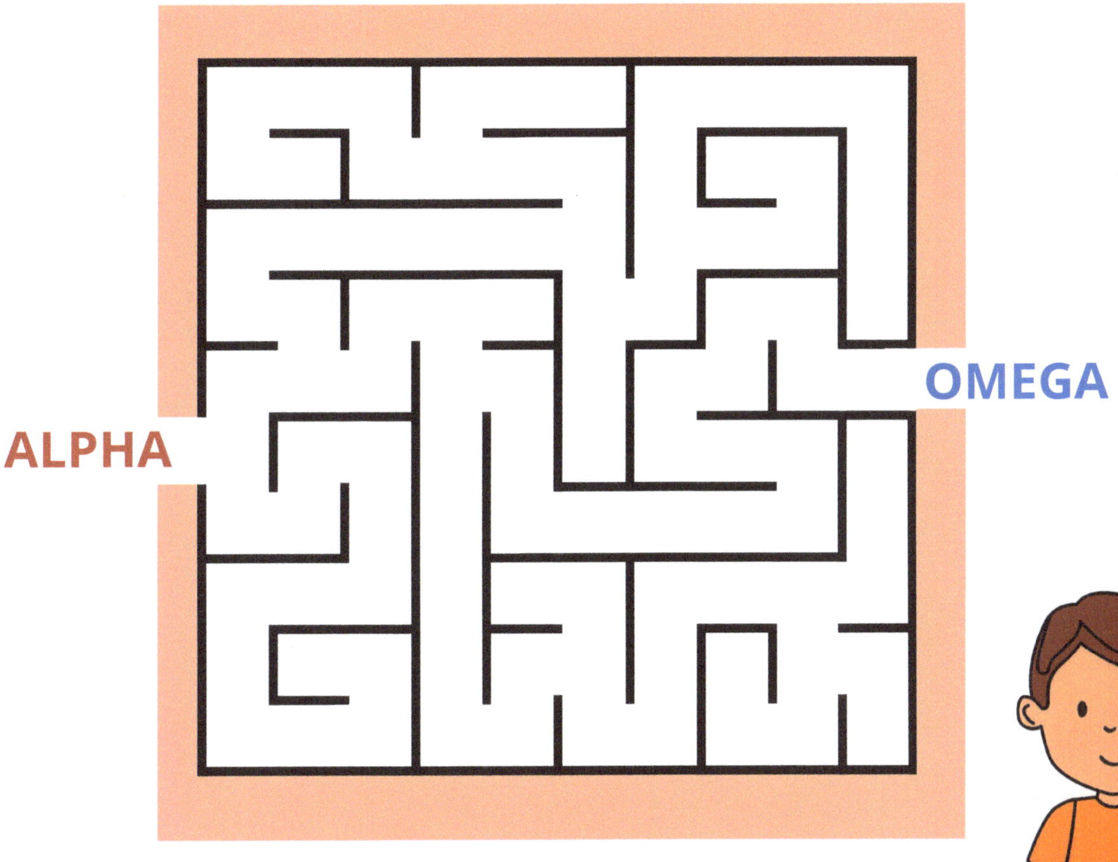

ALPHA → [maze] → **OMEGA**

I am the Alpha and the Omega, the First and the Last, the Beginning and the End.
Revelation 22:13

With all our hearts does not mean that you have more than one heart in your body!

In fact, this phrase reminds us that we are part of a global civilization, each lifting our heart to the Lord, to praise and bless His name together.

When we sing, **"We bless Your name,"** we are saying, "We are praising and worshipping You God, because we know that you are awesome, majestic and sovereign Lord!"

This brings God joy and blesses Him. How incredible that we can do this!

Find these hidden words in the puzzle below:

- LORD
- PRAISE
- ALMIGHTY
- PRESENCE
- PEOPLE
- CREATION
- SING
- BLESS
- LAMB
- NATION
- TRIBE
- HOLY
- AGE
- DECADE
- TIME
- DAY
- MONTH
- YEAR
- ETERNAL
- EVERLASTING

BOOK 6: Holy is the Lamb

A CLOSER LOOK

From every language, tribe and nation Your holy people sing Your praise

There are millions of people living in different communities all across the earth. Their languages are different, their food is different, their homes are different.

God's word says that every tribe and nation will lift their voices in praise to Him.

After this I looked, and there was an enormous crowd—no one could count all the people! They were from every race, tribe, nation, and language, and they stood in front of the throne and of the Lamb, dressed in white robes and holding palm branches in their hands. They called out in a loud voice: "Salvation comes from our God, who sits on the throne, and from the Lamb!"

Revelation 7:9-10

Activity Time

See if you can match the words 'Holy is the Lamb' with the language it is written in. Then draw a flag of a country where this language is spoken.

Holy is the Lamb	Spanish	☐
Santo es el cordero	Japanese	☐
ቅዱስ ነው	Amharic	☐
k'idusi newi	French	☐
Heilig ist das Lamm	English	☐
saint est l'agneau	German	☐
聖なる子羊	isiZulu	☐

HINT: You can look up the flags online if you don't know them!

BOOK 6: Holy is the Lamb

A CLOSER LOOK

We bow before Your holy presence

In some countries and cultures people bow as a sign of respect and submission.

In the same way, we **bow before** the one true King, God - to let Him know how much we respect and submit to Him. After all, He is the King and Ruler of our lives.

Even when we do not physically **bow** before the Lord, we should always bow in our hearts to His will. This shows God that we recognize Him as Lord of all, ALWAYS!

A CLOSER LOOK

We lift our hands and worship You

When **we lift our hands,** we are saying to God, "I give myself to You," or "I surrender to You."

When we **lift our hands and worship** God, we surrender our attention to Him alone.

We give Him our full focus and block out all other distractions around us.

We lift God high, and surrender everything to Him!

BOOK 6: Holy is the Lamb

A CLOSER LOOK

**Lord, You alone deserve this honor
You alone deserve all praise
All praise**

Our worship is an expression of total thankfulness to God, and complete respect for Him.

We also honor our parents and leaders—but our worship is reserved only for God.

Use the secret code to find a hidden phrase from the song.

See if you can use these words the next time you pray.

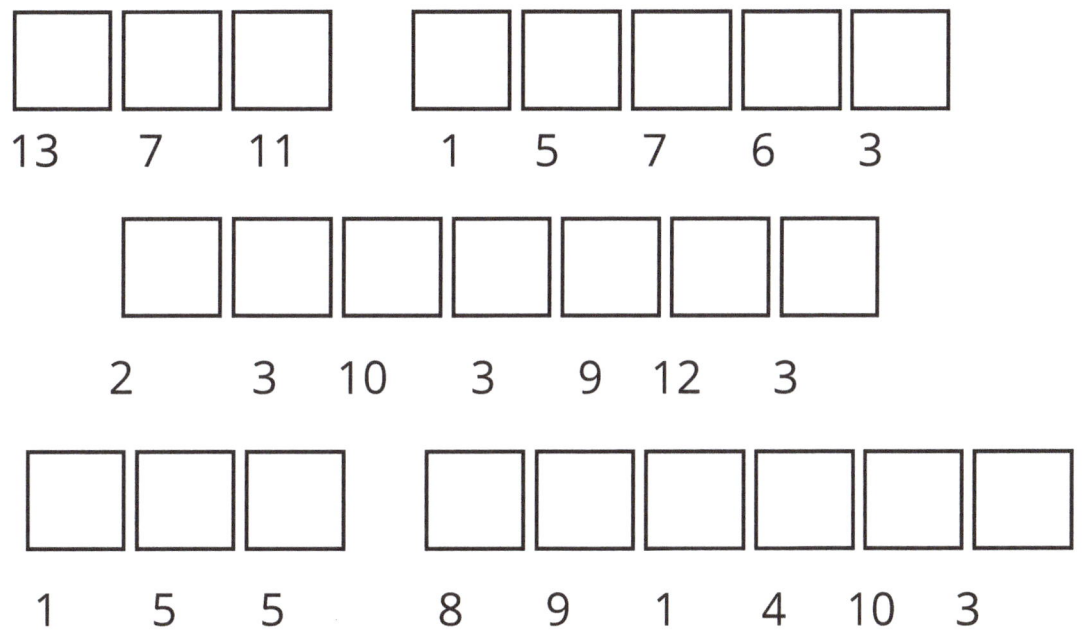

Be sure to share what you discovered!

Secret Code

A	D	E	I	L	N	O	P	R	S	U	V	Y
1	2	3	4	5	6	7	8	9	10	11	12	13

ANSWER: YOU ALONE DESERVE ALL PRAISE

BOOK 6: Holy is the Lamb

> Take some time to reflect on this song. Here's some space to write down your thoughts.

MY JOURNAL

www.ingramcontent.com/pod-product-compliance
Lightning Source LLC
Chambersburg PA
CBHW041123070526
44584CB00002B/257